Andrew Brodie Basics

LET'S DO GRAMMAR

FOR AGES 6-7

with over 100 reward stickers

- Over 50 activities
- Regular progress tests
- Matched to the National Curriculum

Andrew Brodie
An imprint of Bloomsbury Publishing Plc

50 Bedford Square
London
WC1B 3DP
UK

1385 Broadway
New York
NY 10018
USA

www.bloomsbury.com

ANDREW BRODIE is a trademark of Bloomsbury Publishing Plc

First published in Great Britain 2017

Copyright © Andrew Brodie, 2017
Cover and inside illustrations of Andrew Brodie and Pedro the panda © Nikalas Catlow, 2017
All other inside illustrations copyright © Cathy Hughes, 2017

Andrew Brodie has asserted his right under the Copyright, Designs and Patents Act, 1988,
to be identified as Author of this work.

All rights reserved.
No part of this publication may be reproduced or transmitted in any form or by any means,
electronic or mechanical, including photocopying, recording, or any information storage or
retrieval system, without prior permission in writing from the publishers.

No responsibility for loss caused to any individual or organisation acting on or refraining from
action as a result of the material in this publication can be accepted by Bloomsbury or the author.

A catalogue record for this book is available from the British Library.

ISBN
PB: 978-1-4729-4064-3
ePDF: 978-1-4729-4063-6

2 4 6 8 10 9 7 5 3 1

Designed and typeset by Marcus Duck Design
Printed and bound in China by Leo Paper Products

This book is produced using paper that is made from wood grown in managed,
sustainable forests. It is natural, renewable and recyclable. The logging and manufacturing
processes conform to the environmental regulations of the country of origin.

To find out more about our authors and books visit www.bloomsbury.com.
Here you will find extracts, author interviews, details of forthcoming events and the
option to sign up for our newsletters.

BLOOMSBURY

Notes for parents

What's in this book

This is the second in the series of *Andrew Brodie Basics: Let's Do Grammar* books. Each book features a clearly structured approach to developing and improving children's knowledge and use of grammar in their reading and writing as well as in their oral communication.

The National Curriculum states that children in Year 2 should learn appropriate terminology in relation to grammar and punctuation, including the following:
- letter, capital letter
- word, singular, plural, suffix, noun, noun phrase, adjective, verb, adverb, compound
- sentence, statement, question, exclamation, command
- present tense, past tense
- punctuation: full stop, question mark, exclamation mark.*

*Note that in 2016 the Government stated that, in tests, pupils will only gain marks for exclamations that begin with 'what' or 'how'.

Children will learn to:
- create sentences with different forms, such as statements, questions, exclamations and commands
- form nouns using suffixes such as *ment, ness* and *er*
- use adjectives to create expanded noun phrases, e.g. *the red car*
- form adjectives using suffixes such as *er, est, ful* and *less*
- turn adjectives into adverbs through the use of *ly* apply the present and past tenses correctly.

How you can help

Make sure your child is ready for their grammar practice and help them to enjoy it using the activities in this book. If necessary, read through each activity out loud, discussing it so that your child really understands what the writing means.

The answer section at the end of this book can be a useful teaching tool: ask your child to compare their responses to the ones shown. Their answers may not be identical but should include similar information. If your child has made mistakes, help them to learn from them. Remember that the speed at which your child progresses will vary from topic to topic.

Most importantly, enjoy the experience of working with your child and sharing the excitement of learning together.

Look out for...

Pedro the Panda, who will help your child understand what to focus on when working through the activities.

Brodie's Brain Boosters, which feature quick extra activities designed to make your child think, using the skills and knowledge they already have. Can they talk about their experiences using appropriate and interesting vocabulary?

Contents

Nouns

How many nouns can you find on this page?

The little dog is running down the path.

↑ ↑

This is a noun. **This is a noun.**

A noun is the name of something.

Read the words below.

dog ~~little~~ house carry car happy computer likely

best pen breaking roof cinema open great floor

window home construct build

Write each word in the correct column in the table. Two have been done for you.

Noun	Not a noun
dog	little

Brodie's Brain Booster

Look around you. Name lots of things you can see.

Odd one out

Can you find the **odd one out** in each line?
The odd one out is a noun. The first one has
been done for you.

big	bright	(bottle)	busy
carry	eat	explore	kitchen
tree	new	tall	slither
better	plate	live	urgent
only	build	building	far
much	money	marry	modern
nest	never	nearer	naughty
ordering	opener	ordinary	organise

Choose one of the nouns.
Write a really good sentence that includes your chosen noun.

_____

_____

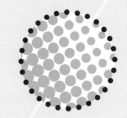

Brodie's Brain Booster

What are the names of the different
rooms in a house? List as many as
you can.

5

Nouns that go together

The word **bamboo** is a noun. I like bamboo.

All the words below are nouns. Write each one in the correct box.

tiger   bathroom   horse   kitchen   sitting room   giraffe

eagle   bus   blackbird   lorry   van   swan

Animals

_____

_____

_____

Rooms

_____

_____

_____

Birds

_____

_____

_____

Vehicles

_____

_____

_____

Brodie's Brain Booster

Can you think of an extra noun for each set?

Finding nouns

Remember, a noun is the name of something.

Draw a ring around each noun in the sentences below.

The cat is chasing the mouse.

The girl ran into the house.

A boy is swimming in the pool.

The car is parked on the drive.

The family moved into their new house.

Brodie's Brain Booster

Can you make up a sentence that includes two nouns?

Hidden nouns

These nouns may be trickier to find.

Look for the nouns.

They may be written across, like this: c a t s

They may be written down, like this:
d
o
g
s

There are ten words to find. One has been done for you.

a	s	l	a	b	l	e	s	c	d
e	f	g	h	r	i	v	e	r	d
m	n	f	c	i	w	s	a	q	s
r	s	r	u	d	v	o	w	x	t
b	o	i	e	g	y	c	z	a	a
b	c	e	l	e	p	h	a	n	t
j	k	n	p	l	a	s	h	e	i
f	u	d	g	e	q	r	s	t	o
a	w	x	t	r	s	p	o	o	n
n	i	n	s	a	b	c	d	e	f

Checklist:

- bridge ✓
- fan
- station
- slab
- sea
- river
- fudge
- elephant
- spoon
- friend

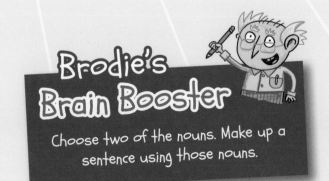

Brodie's **Brain Booster**

Choose two of the nouns. Make up a sentence using those nouns.

Nouns in sentences

Don't forget that each sentence starts with a capital letter.

Look back at the nouns you found on page 8. Choose four of the nouns and make up a sentence using each one. You may use more than one noun in each sentence.

Draw a picture to go with one of your sentences.

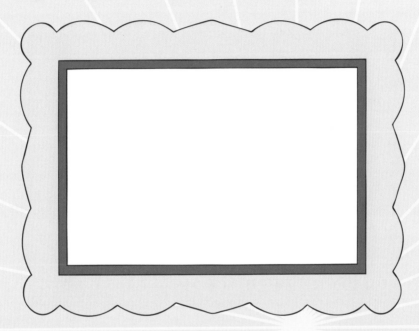

1. _____

_____

2. _____

_____

3. _____

_____

4. _____

_____

Did you remember to put a full stop at the end of each sentence?

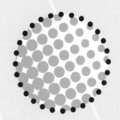

Can you find the odd one out in each line?
Hint: each odd one out is a noun. The first one has been done for you.

wonderful	(barn)	happy	warm
enjoy	icy	nosy	monkey
knee	knock	know	knit
wrap	parcel	unwrap	give
moving	adjust	improve	taxi

Draw a ring around each noun in the sentences below.

The child is driving the tractor.

The rain is falling from the sky.

My dad is baking a cake.

Write a sentence about an animal. Draw a ring around each noun in your sentence.

_____

_____

_____

Singular means that there is just one person or thing. Plural means that there is more than one.

one fox

three foxes

The word **fox** is a singular noun.

The word **foxes** is a plural noun.

When a word ends in **ch**, **sh**, **s**, **ss**, **x** or **z**, we add an **e** before the final **s** to make it mean more than one (plural). Change these singular nouns to plural nouns.

animal _____   bus _____

floor _____   dish _____

door _____   hutch _____

river _____   day _____

match _____   dress _____

box _____   church _____

Write a sentence that includes a plural noun.

_____

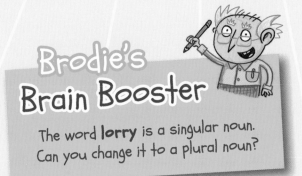

Brodie's Brain Booster

The word **lorry** is a singular noun. Can you change it to a plural noun?

Changing endings

Did you know that the ending of some nouns need to be changed to make them plural?

 one lorry  three lorries

The word **lorry** is a singular noun.

The word **lorries** is a plural noun.

**Change these singular nouns to plural nouns.
They each need y removed before you add ies.**

pony _____   jelly _____

copy _____   flurry _____

baby _____   diary _____

lady _____   party _____

poppy _____   city _____

 one mouse

three mice

The word **mouse** is a singular noun.

The word **mice** is a plural noun.

**Change these singular nouns to plural nouns.
These nouns all need to be changed in different ways.**

mouse _____   child _____

goose _____   man _____

tooth _____   woman _____

Find the plural nouns

Can you find all the plural nouns?

Look for the plural words.

They may be written across, like this: m i c e

They may be written down, like this: d
o
o
r
s

There are ten words to find. One has been done for you.

m	i	c	e	b	l	e	s	c	d
e	f	h	h	o	i	j	k	l	d
m	n	i	g	h	t	s	p	q	i
r	s	l	u	o	v	o	w	x	s
b	o	d	e	u	y	d	z	a	h
d	c	r	e	s	h	o	p	s	e
o	k	e	p	e	a	o	h	h	s
l	i	n	e	s	q	r	s	e	u
l	w	x	t	r	e	s	s	e	z
s	r	n	s	a	b	c	d	p	f

Checklist:

- children ✓
- dishes
- dolls
- mice
- lines
- shops
- houses
- sheep
- doors
- nights

Brodie's Brain Booster

Choose one of the words. Make up a sentence using that word. Can you write the sentence down?

13

Making nouns using ment

Did you know that some nouns can be made from other words?

Does the girl enjoy climbing the tree?
The girl gets enjoyment from climbing the tree.

Did you notice that the word enjoyment can be made from enjoy?
The ending ment is called a suffix.

Look at the words below.
Make them into nouns by adding the suffix ment.

enjoy _____   assess _____

pay _____   equip _____

move _____   assort _____

appoint _____   govern _____

Brodie's Brain Booster

Do you remember the special name for endings that can be added to words?

Making nouns using ness

Nouns can be made by adding the suffix ness to some words.

The boy was kind to the man who had fallen over.
The man thanked the boy for his kindness.

Did you notice that the word kindness can be made from kind?
The ending ness is called a suffix.

Look at the words below.
Make them into nouns by adding the suffix ness.

kind _____   weak _____

fresh _____   ill _____

sad _____   dark _____

shy _____   good _____

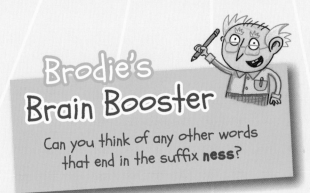

Brodie's Brain Booster

Can you think of any other words that end in the suffix **ness**?

Making nouns using er

Nouns can be made by adding the suffix er to some words.

The girl can drive the tractor.
The girl is a tractor driver.

Did you notice that the word driver can be made from drive?
The ending er is called a suffix.

Look at the words below.
Make them into nouns by adding the suffix er.
If the word ends in an e, you only have to add the r from er.

drive _____   blend _____

camp _____   scoot _____

build _____   save _____

walk _____   spend _____

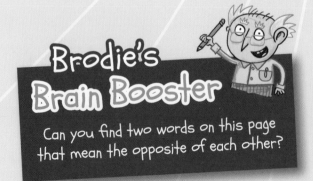

Brodie's Brain Booster

Can you find two words on this page that mean the opposite of each other?

Change these singular nouns to plural nouns.

road _____   mountain _____

potato _____   domino _____

driver _____   wish _____

machine _____   buzz _____

tooth _____   child _____

shoulder _____   hand _____

ash _____   mouse _____

splash _____

Look at the words below.
Make them into nouns by adding the suffixes ment or ness or er.

tired _____   climb _____

judge _____   enjoy _____

buzz _____   talk _____

sad _____   teach _____

assort _____

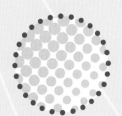

Adjectives

The **little** dog is running down the path.

This is a noun.   This is a noun.

This is an adjective. It tells us something about the dog. It's a **little** dog.

Draw a ring around each adjective in the sentences below.

The black cat is chasing the little mouse.

The big girl has a long rope.

The young boy ate a huge biscuit.

The yellow bird flew into the tall tree.

Brodie's Brain Booster

Can you make up a sentence that includes an adjective?

Nouns and adjectives

Make some noun phrases by putting adjectives with nouns.

Adjective Bank:

big   little   hungry   tall   short   narrow

Noun Bank:

cat   mouse   road   elephant   city   tree

Write some noun phrases using the words in the Banks. Each noun phrase needs an adjective with a noun. There are lots you can make. One is done for you.

 a big cat

_____

_____   _____

_____   _____

_____   _____

_____   _____

_____   _____

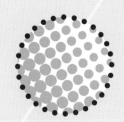

Brodie's Brain Booster
Use two of your noun phrases in a sentence.

You can change some adjectives by adding the suffix **er**.

This is Herbie. Herbie is a small dog. This is Hamish. Hamish is a big dog.

Herbie is smaller than Hamish. Hamish is bigger than Herbie.

Look how small changes to smaller by adding the suffix er.

Look how big changes to bigger. To add the suffix er an extra g had to be added.

Change these adjectives into new adjectives by adding the suffix er.

thick _____   neat _____

wet _____   sharp _____

rich _____   kind _____

poor _____   bright _____

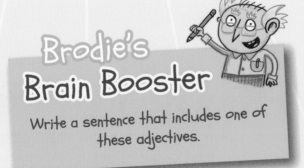

Brodie's Brain Booster

Write a sentence that includes one of these adjectives.

Changing adjectives by adding est

You can change some adjectives by adding the suffix **est**.

This is Herbie. Herbie is a small dog.

This is Hamish. Hamish is a big dog.

This is Kizzy. Kizzy is very big.

Herbie is smaller than Hamish. Hamish is bigger than Herbie. Kizzy is the biggest dog.

Look how small changes to smaller by adding the suffix er.

Look how big changes to bigger. To add the suffix er an extra g had to be added.

Look how big changes to biggest. To add the suffix est an extra g had to be added.

Change these adjectives into new adjectives by adding the suffix est.

narrow _____ poor _____

tight _____ tall _____

smart _____ short _____

rich _____ thin _____

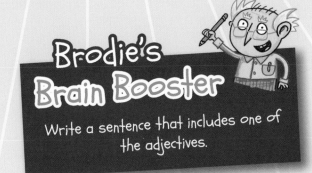

Brodie's Brain Booster

Write a sentence that includes one of the adjectives.

Changing adjectives by adding ful

Take care.

I'm being very careful.

You can change some adjectives by adding the suffix **ful**.

Look how care changes to careful by adding the suffix **ful**.

Change these adjectives into new adjectives by adding the suffix **ful**.

care _____   use _____

wonder _____   cheer _____

help _____   delight _____

hope _____   pain _____

What a beautiful day!

Look how you can change beauty to **beautiful** by adding the suffix **ful**. Did you notice that the letter **y** has been replaced with a letter **i**?

Change these adjectives into new adjectives by adding the suffix **ful**.

beauty _____

pity _____

bounty _____

mercy _____

plenty _____

Brodie's Brain Booster

Write a sentence that includes one of the adjectives.

You can change some adjectives by adding the suffix **less**.

You were not very careful.

I was quite careless really.

Change these adjectives into new adjectives by adding the suffix less.

care _____   aim _____

help _____   cord _____

hope _____   effort _____

use _____   point _____

pain _____   thought _____

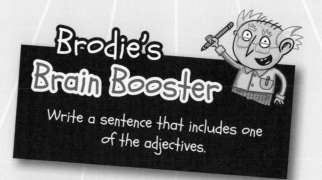

Brodie's
Brain Booster

Write a sentence that includes one of the adjectives.

23

Make some noun phrases by putting each adjective with a noun.

Adjective Bank: careful careless beautiful sweetest wonderful tiniest

Noun Bank: afternoon cat cake baby driver climber

_____   _____

_____   _____

_____   _____

Find the adjectives.
There are ten to find. One has been done for you.

m	b	i	g	g	e	r	s	c	d
e	f	h	h	o	i	j	u	l	d
c	a	r	e	l	e	s	s	q	h
r	s	l	u	d	v	o	e	x	e
b	o	d	n	e	e	d	f	u	l
d	s	r	e	n	h	o	u	s	p
o	h	e	p	e	a	o	l	h	l
d	a	m	p	s	w	r	s	e	e
l	r	x	t	r	e	s	s	e	s
s	p	o	i	n	t	l	e	s	s

Checklist:
- bigger ✓
- damp
- useful
- pointless
- careless
- needful
- helpless
- sharp
- wet
- golden

Choose one of the adjectives and use it in a sentence. Write your sentence here.

_____

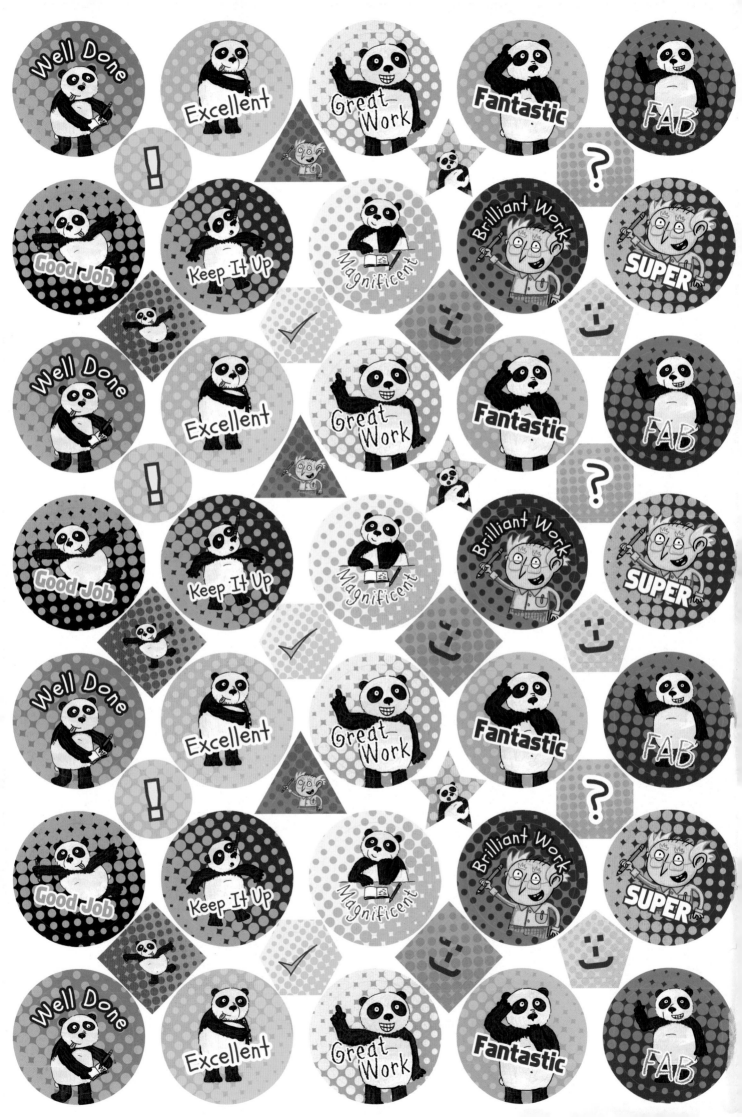

Every sentence includes a verb.

The dogs run down the path.

This is a verb. It tells us what the dogs are doing.

A verb often tells us what someone or something is doing.

Be a verb detective. Draw a ring around the verb in each sentence.

We walk to school.

The birds eat the food.

The girls play football.

Sometimes the verb needs the suffix s.

The boy draws a picture.

The verb is draw but we have to write draws.

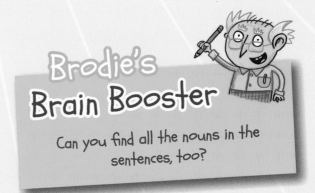

Brodie's Brain Booster

Can you find all the nouns in the sentences, too?

More about verbs

A verb may need the help of other words.

The girl is climbing a tree.

The word **is** helps the verb **climbing**.

The word **climbing** is a verb. It is made from the verb **climb**.

Circle each verb in the sentences below.

The dogs are chasing the cat.

The cat is frightening the dogs.

The car is moving fast.

The tree is falling down.

The adults are drinking coffee.

The builder is laying some bricks.

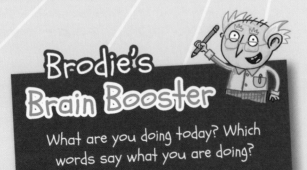

Brodie's Brain Booster

What are you doing today? Which words say what you are doing?

26

Even more about verbs

Verbs often need suffixes.

The girl is climbing a tree.

The suffix ing has been added to the verb climb.

Sometimes an e needs to be removed before ing is added.

The girl is driving the tractor. Driving is made from the verb drive.

Add the suffix ing to the verbs. Some words will need e removed first.

talk _____   paint _____

watch _____   listen _____

write _____   hide _____

draw _____   work _____

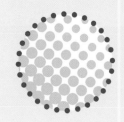

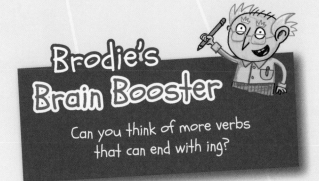

Brodie's Brain Booster

Can you think of more verbs that can end with ing?

27

Criss-cross verbs

Read the words below:

copy ride move join ~~read~~ visit sweep

joining riding moving visiting copying ~~reading~~ sweeping

improving enjoy improve finding enjoying find

Write the words in the criss-cross boxes. Each criss-cross should contain a pair of verbs. One has been done for you.

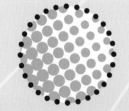

Brodie's Brain Booster

Write a sentence using one of your **ing** verbs.

28

The past tense

We use verbs when we write about things that have already happened.

The boy played football yesterday.

This sentence tells us what the boy did yesterday.
Yesterday is in the past.

The verb played is in the past tense.

The suffix ed has been added to the verb play.

Change these verbs to the past tense by adding the suffix ed.

climb _____   walk _____

enjoy _____   talk _____

invent _____   connect _____

Write a sentence using one of the ed verbs.

_____

_____

Brodie's
Brain Booster

What is the past tense of the verb blow?

Strange past tense verbs

We don't add **ed** to some verbs when we make the past tense. We sometimes need to change other letters too.

The boys blow up the balloons.

This verb is in the present tense.

The boys blew up the balloons.

This verb is in the past tense.

Write the past tense of all the verbs below. Some will need ed added. Some will need to be changed in a different way instead.

know _____ dig _____

change _____ paint _____

yawn _____ break _____

drive _____ write _____

build _____ mix _____

Write a sentence using one of the past tense verbs.

_____

_____

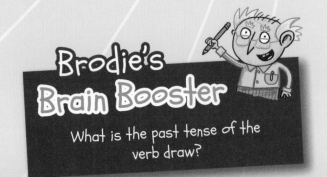

Brodie's Brain Booster

What is the past tense of the verb draw?

Can you find the odd one out in each line? The odd one out is a verb. The first one has been done for you.

yesterday	tomorrow	(running)	warm
climbed	mountain	hill	forest
yellow	drew	picture	sketch
following	leader	friend	friendly
top	red	blue	stopping
jumper	shoulder	jumped	elbow
silver	shivered	river	liver

Write two sentences about what you did at the weekend. Draw a ring around each verb you used.

_____

_____

_____

_____

Adverbs

Adverbs are words that often go with verbs.

The children are reading quietly.

This is the verb. It tells us what the children are doing.

This is the adverb. It tells us how the children are reading.

Use a red crayon and a blue crayon. Use the red crayon to draw a ring around each verb. Use the blue crayon to draw a ring around each adverb.

The birds are singing loudly.

Mum was speaking quickly.

Dad climbed the ladder carefully.

Here are some adverbs. badly softly cheerfully

Write a sentence using one of these adverbs.

_____

_____

Brodie's
Brain Booster

Can you make an adverb from the adjective narrow?

Adverbs from adjectives

Make some adverbs from the adjectives using the suffix **ly**.

**Write an adverb next to each adjective.
The first one is done for you.**

brave   _bravely_   sharp _____

kind   _____   short _____

nice   _____   narrow _____

proud   _____   thick _____

careful   _____   wide _____

Write a sentence using one of the adverbs you have made.

_____

_____

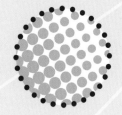

Brodie's Brain Booster

Can you make an adverb from the adjective happy?

Making more adverbs

Some adjectives need to be changed when they are made into adverbs.

The baby is happy. She is smiling happily.

This adjective ends with the letter y.

The y has been replaced with an i so that ly could be added.

Write an adverb next to each adjective. The first one is done for you.

happy	*happily*	funny	_____
snappy	_____	messy	_____
shabby	_____	merry	_____
soggy	_____	crazy	_____
busy	_____		

Write a sentence using one of the adverbs you have made.

_____

_____

Brodie's Brain Booster

Can you make an adverb from the word gentle?

34

Find the adverbs

Can you find all the adverbs?

Look for the adverbs.
They may be written across, like this: s o f t l y
They may be written down, like this:
d
r
e
a
m
i
l
y

There are seven adverbs to find. One has been done for you.

d	i	c	e	b	l	e	g	s	d
r	o	u	g	h	l	y	k	o	d
e	n	i	g	a	t	s	p	f	i
a	s	p	u	p	a	b	c	t	e
m	o	r	e	p	o	o	r	l	y
i	c	o	e	i	h	o	p	y	e
l	o	u	d	l	y	o	h	h	s
y	i	d	e	y	q	r	s	e	u
l	w	l	t	r	e	s	s	e	z
s	i	y	s	a	b	c	d	p	f

Checklist:

- dreamily ✓
- softly
- poorly
- proudly
- loudly
- happily
- roughly

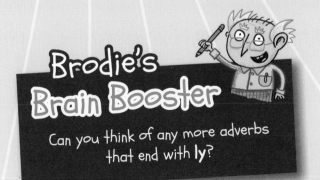

Brodie's Brain Booster

Can you think of any more adverbs that end with **ly**?

Climbing a tree

I climb trees very carefully.

The adverb doesn't have to be next to the verb.

Can you find all the adverbs in this story? Be careful, not all the sentences include an adverb.

Jess was climbing up the tree carefully. Suddenly a branch broke. Jess fell down quickly. She landed on the ground with a hard bump. She stood up and wiped the leaves off roughly. She began to climb the tree slowly.

Write the adverbs that you found.

_____   _____

_____   _____

_____

Write down some of the verbs in the story.

_____   _____

_____

Write down some of the nouns in the story.

_____   _____

_____

There is only one adjective. Can you find it?

_____

Brodie's
Brain Booster

Can you think of a short story to write?

Writing a short story

Your story will include nouns and verbs.

Write a short story. Try to include some adverbs and adjectives. You can also draw a picture to go with the story.

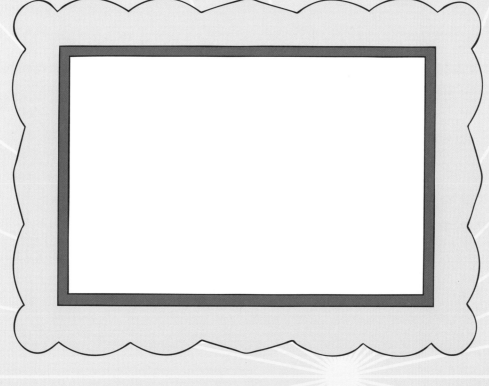

_____

_____

_____

_____

_____

_____

_____

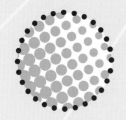

Brodie's Brain Booster

How many adverbs did you use?

Use a red crayon and a blue crayon.
Use the red crayon to draw a ring around each verb.
Use the blue crayon to draw a ring around each adverb.

The rain is falling heavily.

The bell is ringing loudly.

The wind is blowing softly.

Make some adverbs from the adjectives using the suffix ly.
Write an adverb next to each adjective.

strong _____   quick _____

weak _____   quiet _____

neat _____

Now try these.

noisy _____   bossy _____

hungry _____   funny _____

angry _____

Questions

Can I go swimming?

Every question sentence ends with a question mark.

Did you notice the question mark in the speech bubble?

Oh look, there's another one.

Think about some questions you could ask a friend. They could be about your friend's holiday. They could be about your friend's family or pets. Write the question sentences below.

_____

_____

_____

_____

_____

_____

Brodie's
Brain Booster

Ask your friend to answer your questions. Write down the replies.

Statements

Statements are sentences that tell you something.

Here are some statements.

Today is Wednesday.

My birthday is in January.

I go swimming on Tuesdays.

Write some statements about you and your family.

Lots of sentences are statements.

_____

_____

_____

_____

_____

_____

_____

_____

Brodie's Brain Booster

Look in your reading book. Can you find a question and a statement?

Exclamations

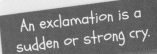

An exclamation is a sudden or strong cry.

Exclamations often start with the words what or how.

Here are some exclamations.

What super work!

How beautiful!

Did you notice the exclamation marks?

Be careful, because questions often start with the words what or how too.

Here are some questions.

What are you doing?

How are you going to write your story?

Here is another exclamation. Look at the exclamation mark.

How strong you are!

Write some exclamations about the weather today.

_____

_____

_____

_____

_____

Brodie's Brain Booster

Look in your reading book. Can you find an exclamation mark? Did the exclamation start with what or how?

Commands

A command tells you what to do.

Parents and teachers often give commands. Sometimes they are quite short sentences.

Here are some commands.

Tidy your room.

Finish your work.

Pick up your pencil.

Clean your teeth.

Imagine you have a robot that will do everything you want. Write some commands for your robot.

_____

_____

_____

_____

_____

_____

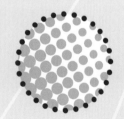

Brodie's Brain Booster

Has anybody told you what to do today? Can you remember the commands they used?

Sentence detective

Can you become a sentence detective?

Come with me.

Where are we going?

I want to show you my new room.

How lucky you are!

Identify each of the sentences. Write each one out below the correct title.

Statement

_____

Question

_____

Exclamation

_____

Command

_____

Brodie's Brain Booster

There are two adjectives in the four sentences. Can you find them?

It's your turn to write the four types of sentences.

Write three statements.

_____

_____

_____

Write two questions.

_____

_____

_____

Write two commands.

_____

_____

_____

Write one exclamation.

_____

_____

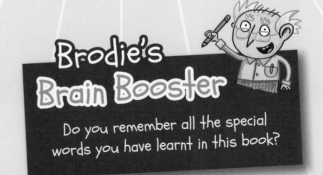

Brodie's Brain Booster

Do you remember all the special words you have learnt in this book?

What do you want to do today?

Take me to the beach.

How cheeky you are!

I am always cheeky.

Identify each of the sentences. Write each one out below the correct title.

Statement

_____

Question

_____

Exclamation

_____

Command

_____

ANSWERS

Use the answers to check your child's progress but also to give prompts and ideas if they are needed. Note that sometimes your child's answer may not match the answer given here but could be just as good!

p4

Noun	Not a noun
dog	little
house	carry
car	happy
roof	likely
cinema	best
pen	breaking
computer	open
window	great
home	build
floor	construct

Brain Booster

Your child may suggest lots of things that they can see in the room where they are working. Ensure that they understand that each naming word is a noun.

p5

big bright **bottle** busy

carry eat explore **kitchen**

tree new tall slither

better **plate** live urgent

only build **building** far

much **money** marry modern

nest never nearer naughty

ordering **opener** ordinary organize

Check that your child's sentence includes one of the nouns. Does it start with a capital letter and end with a full stop?

Brain Booster

Your child should state the names of rooms in the house: kitchen, sitting room, bathroom, toilet, etc.

p6

Animals: horse giraffe tiger eagle

Rooms: kitchen bathroom sitting room

Birds: blackbird swan eagle

Vehicles: lorry van bus

Brain Booster

Your child will make suggestions for an extra item for each set.

p7

cat, mouse, girl, house, boy, pool, car, drive, family, house

Brain Booster

Encourage your child to make up a clear sentence that includes two nouns.

p8

a	s	l	a	b	l	e	s	c	d
e	f	g	h	r	i	v	e	r	d
m	n	f	c	i	w	s	a	q	s
r	s	r	u	d	v	o	w	x	t
b	o	i	e	g	y	c	z	a	a
b	c	e	l	e	p	h	a	n	t
j	k	n	p	l	a	s	h	e	i
f	u	d	g	e	q	r	s	t	o
a	w	x	t	r	s	p	o	o	n
n	i	n	s	a	b	c	d	e	f

Brain Booster

Help your child to compose a well-structured sentence.

p9

Your child should compose four appropriate sentences. Remind them to start each one with a capital letter and to end it with a full stop.

Progress Test 1

How well does your child remember what they have practised?

wonderful **barn** happy warm

enjoy icy nosy **monkey**

knee knock know knit

wrap **parcel** unwrap give

moving adjust improve **taxi**

The **child** is driving the **tractor**.

The **rain** is falling from the **sky**.

My **dad** is baking a **cake**.

Your child should write an appropriate sentence and draw rings around the nouns.

p11

animals floors doors rivers matches boxes buses dishes hutches days dresses churches

Help your child to compose a well-structured sentence.

Brain Booster

lorries

p12

ponies copies babies ladies poppies jellies flurries diaries parties cities

mice geese teeth children men women

p13

m	i	c	e	b	l	e	s	c	d
e	f	h	h	o	i	j	k	l	d
m	n	i	g	h	t	s	p	q	i
r	s	l	u	o	v	o	w	x	s
b	o	d	e	u	y	d	z	a	h
d	c	r	e	s	h	o	p	s	e
o	k	e	p	e	a	o	h	h	s
l	i	n	e	s	q	r	s	e	u
l	w	x	t	r	e	s	s	e	z
s	r	n	s	a	b	c	d	p	f

Brain Booster

Your child should compose an appropriate sentence using one of the plural words.

 p14

enjoyment payment movement appointment assessment equipment assortment government

Brain Booster

suffix

 p15

kindness freshness sadness shyness weakness illness darkness goodness

Brain Booster

Encourage your child to think of more words that end with 'ness'.

 p16

driver camper builder walker blender scooter saver spender

Brain Booster

saver spender

Progress Test 2

roads potatoes drivers machines teeth shoulders ashes splashes mountains dominoes wishes buzzes children hands mice

tiredness judgement buzzer sadness assortment climber enjoyment talker teacher

 p18

black, little, big, long, little, huge, yellow, tall

Brain Booster

Help your child to compose a sentence containing a suitable adjective.

 p19

There are lots of noun phrases that can be made. Examples: a big cat, a big mouse, a big elephant, a big city, a big tree, a little cat, a little mouse, a hungry cat, a hungry elephant, a tall elephant, a tall tree, a narrow road.

Brain Booster

Help your child to compose a sentence containing two of the noun phrases. Example: A big cat climbed a tall tree.

 p20

thicker wetter richer poorer neater sharper kinder brighter

Brain Booster

Help your child to compose a sentence that includes one of the adjectives.

 p21

narrowest tightest smartest richest poorest tallest shortest thinnest

Brain Booster

Help your child to compose a sentence that includes one of the adjectives.

 p22

careful wonderful helpful hopeful useful cheerful delightful painful

beautiful pitiful bountiful merciful plentiful

Note that some of these words will be new to your child – discuss the words with them giving them examples of when the words could be used.

Brain Booster

Encourage your child to compose an appropriate sentence.

p23

careless helpless hopeless useless painless aimless cordless effortless pointless thoughtless

Brain Booster

Encourage your child to compose an appropriate sentence.

Progress Test 3

There are lots of noun phrases that can be made. Examples: a careful driver a careless driver a beautiful baby a wonderful afternoon a careful climber the sweetest cake

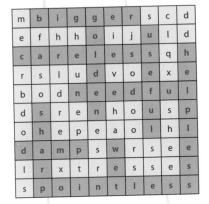

Encourage your child to compose an appropriate sentence.

 p25

walk eat play

Brain Booster

dogs path we (this may not be an easy noun to find as it is a pronoun) school birds food girls football boy picture

 p26

chasing frightening moving falling drinking laying

Brain Booster

Can your child think of ing verbs about the day's activities?

 p27

talking watching writing drawing painting listening hiding working

Brain Booster

Discuss lots of verbs ending with ing.

 p28

read reading
sweep, sweeping
copy copying
join joining
visit visiting
ride riding
move moving
improve improving
find finding
enjoy enjoying

Brain Booster

Help your child to think of an appropriate sentence.

 p29

climbed enjoyed invented walked talked connected

Your child should compose a suitable sentence in the past tense.

Brain Booster

blew

p30

knew changed yawned drove built dug painted broke wrote mixed (To find some of these, encourage your child to try to say each word in a sentence.)

Brain Booster

drew

yesterday tomorrow **running** warm

climbed mountain hill forest

yellow **drew** picture sketch

following leader friend friendly

top red blue **stopping**

jumper shoulder **jumped** elbow

silver **shivered** river liver

Your child should write appropriate sentences and find the verbs they've used.

p32

red rings: singing speaking climbed
blue rings: loudly quickly carefully

Help your child to compose and write a sentence that includes one of the adverbs.

Brain Booster

narrowly

p33

kindly nicely proudly carefully sharply shortly narrowly thickly widely

Help your child to compose and write a sentence that includes one of the adverbs.

Brain Booster

happily

p34

snappily shabbily soggily busily funnily messily merrily crazily

Your child should write a sentence using one of the adverbs. Check that there is a capital letter at the start and a full stop at the end.

Brain Booster

gently

p35

d	i	c	e	b	l	e	g	s	d
r	o	u	g	h	l	y	k	o	d
e	n	i	g	a	t	s	p	f	i
a	s	p	u	p	a	b	c	t	e
m	o	r	e	p	o	o	r	l	y
i	c	o	e	i	h	o	p	y	e
l	o	u	d	l	y	o	h	h	s
y	i	d	e	y	q	r	s	e	u
l	w	l	t	r	e	s	s	e	z
s	i	y	s	a	b	c	d	p	f

Brain Booster

Encourage your child to think of more adverbs that end with ly.

p36

adverbs: carefully suddenly quickly roughly slowly

Three of the following verbs: climbing broke fell landed stood wiped began climb

Three of the following nouns: Jess (your child may not find this proper noun) tree branch she (pronoun) ground bump leaves

adjective: hard

Brain Booster

Help your child to think of a short story.

p37

Your child should write out the story that you talked about together. Encourage them to use adjectives and adverbs.

Brain Booster

Can your child find all the adverbs they have used?

red rings: falling ringing blowing
blue rings: heavily loudly softly

strongly weakly neatly quickly quietly noisily hungrily angrily bossily funnily

p39

Your child should compose some questions, remembering to start each one with a capital letter and to end each one with a question mark.

Brain Booster

You could be the friend who answers the questions.

p40

Your child should compose some statements, remembering to start each one with a capital letter and to end each one with a full stop.

Brain Booster

Can your child find a question and a statement in the reading book?

p41

Your child should compose some exclamations, remembering to start each one with a capital letter and to end each one with an exclamation mark.

Brain Booster

Can your child find an exclamation mark in the reading book? The exclamation may not start with what or how.

p42

Check that your child has written appropriate commands.

Brain Booster

Talk about commands that your child has been given today.

p43

Statement: I want to show you my new room.

Question: Where are we going?

Exclamation: How lucky you are!

Command: Come with me.

Brain Booster

new lucky

p44

Help your child to write the appropriate sentences.

Brain Booster

Vocabulary includes: noun, noun phrase, adjective, verb, adverb, statement, question, exclamation, command, past tense

Statement: I am always cheeky.

Question: What do you want to do today?

Exclamation: How cheeky you are!

Command: Take me to the beach.